People
&
Places

Pictures by Phoenix Photos

People
&
Places

Pictures by Phoenix Photos

A photographic archive
by Dougie Shearer
of Phoenix Photos

Text researched and compiled
by G. D. Partner

Published 2001

ISBN 1 902957 15 6

The publishers are grateful to the staff of The Orkney Photographic Archive
for their assistance in the production of *People & Places*

Printed and published by
The Orcadian Limited
Hell's Half Acre, Hatston, Kirkwall,
Orkney, Scotland, KW15 1DW

Telephone 01856 879000
Fax 01856 879001
www.orcadian.co.uk

Introduction

It is probably not surprising that Dougie Shearer took a keen interest in everything to do with films and images; be they movies, "talkies", or still photographs....

He was born at 43 Albert Street in the heart of Kirkwall, and for many years was within a dozen or so paces of the Albert Kinema. Not only were the latest films within easy access but he also qualified for free admission, since the Kinema was run by his grandfather, D.B Peace, the founder of cinema in Orkney.

Dougie left Kirkwall Grammar School at the earliest opportunity to join his grandfather in the business and he has many happy memories of his early working life. He grew up to become manager of the Kinema on behalf of the Shearer family but disaster struck in 1947 when the building was gutted by a devastating fire.

However, eight years later the family ambitiously opened a brand new cinema in Junction Road. It was aptly named the Phoenix and weekly film shows were shown there for around 30 years before the Orkney Islands Council took it over.

Dougie created Phoenix Photos after the retiral of James W. Sinclair, the well-known Orkney photographer, and this book reflects the wide variety of events he captured on film during the very late 60s, 70s and 80s. Latterly, his nephew, Donald, who is actually pictured as a young boy in *People and Places*, assisted him.

In addition to photography, music is the love of Dougie's life and he played fiddle for more than 40 years in countless local musical productions. For 16 years he also combined his photographic duties with a full time music teaching job at Kirkwall Grammar School and several rural schools.

Today, at the grand age of 88, he still lives at 43 Albert Street, his birthplace, and is often seen "on the street".

To my sisters

• 1983 •

Brigadier Malcolm G. Dennison, Lord Lieutenant of Orkney 1990-96, is seen here after arriving home in Orkney in March 1983 on his retirement from a career in Oman, having been flown to Kirkwall on board a Hercules transport aircraft of the Omani Air Force. The Hercules was used to fly his furniture home. Though Brig Dennison was born in Nyasaland in 1924 his father came from Shapinsay and his mother from Roeberry, South Ronaldsay and he grew up in Orkney. After graduation from Edinburgh University and war service in Bomber Command RAF, he joined the Sultan of Oman's Armed Forces in 1955 where he served as Director of Intelligence, and then as adviser to the Sultan until his retiral in 1983. In 1976 Brig Dennison became the first Orcadian to fly in Concorde, flying from Heathrow to Bahrein en route to Oman.

• 1977 •

Steam Engine, Harbour Street. Three Kirkwall businessmen, Ron Spiers, Eric MacLennan, and William Johnston formed a consortium to bring this engine to Orkney, obtain the railway tracks from Lyness which are a relic of the past there, and re-lay them in Orphir and run the engine on it. Assistance was sought from the Islands Council but when this was not forthcoming the engine was sold again. This picture shows it on its trailer outside The Girnel en route to the Scottish mainland, where it ended up at the Strathspey Railway Museum. The Girnel itself is one of the oldest buildings in Kirkwall, dating back to approximately 1647. It was the receptacle for the oats, bere, meal and malt which are paid annually as rent in kind by the tenants of the earl. Today it is the home of the Orkney Sailing Club.

• 1977 •

Steam Engine, Craigiefield. This picture shows the steam engine being loaded on to a trailer to begin its journey back to the Scottish mainland. The engine which had belonged to the SSEB had been brought to Orkney a few months previously by three local businessmen, and had lain at Craigiefield pending attempts to create a short railway line in Orphir. The engine was built by Barclay's (Kilmarnock) and was a shunter type 0-4-0 running on Standard Gauge (4 feet 7½ inches) and was blue in colour. On its arrival in Orkney, Stromness Primary pupils were given a half-day off to see it arrive.

• c.1976 •

This aerial view of Kirkwall shows a Loganair aircraft above the town before many of the changes of the '80s and '90s, especially around the pier and harbour area, Hatston, and Kiln Corner took place. Some other features to spot are the old Scout Hall in Willow Road, and, in the lower left-hand side, the bottom corner of the Boys' playground of the old Kirkwall Grammar School. Readers will probably pick out other aspects of interest. The Kiln Corner takes its name form the kiln which was built on the west end of the girnel house for the proper handling of the corn paid as rent at the girnel.

• c.1976 •

This shot gives a closer view of Kirkwall's sea-front in the late '70s. In the inner harbour (the "Basin") the Corn Slip and the slip at the West Pier are still visible. The latter disappeared after the Harbour Street alterations in the 1990s and the Corn Slip was shortened from the shore side by the widening of Harbour Street. The Ayre Road shoreline before land reclamation and the construction of the Shapinsay ferry terminal can also be clearly seen, as can the sheds on the east side of the pier from the "Basin" and the small car park near the harbour office. Land reclamation along Shore Street created the current parking area, and the pier itself has been lengthened and given a new direction to accommodate larger ships. The vessel on the east side at the point of the pier could be the *St Clement*, while on the other side the *Orcadia* is berthed.

• Early 1960s •

Generations of Kirkwall youngsters used to fish off the Corn Slip with a simple rod, line and hook for "sillocks," very small young cuithes (properly coalfish). Youngsters also rowed about the inner harbour ("Basin"). This picture is a fine example of these activities. Featured in the foreground are Wilson Learmonth and Anne Rousay.

In the rear of the rowing boat is Donald Shearer, Dougie's nephew, who eventually assisted him with Phoenix Photos. In the background is the *Orcadia* and the *Amelia* stores. The stores have been demolished and storage tanks stand in their place and the marshalling area for cars travelling on the North Isles ferries.

• c.1969 •

This aerial view is another fine study of Kirkwall and its harbour area before the renovations and extensions. At the west side of the North Pier lie three vessels — the *Islander* with the flags (probably the day she arrived to take over from the *Earl Sigurd*), the *Orcadia* behind her, and the *Sigurd* at the rear. At the north point of the pier (the extreme left) is the light which was removed. Also seen clearly are the eastern and western extensions to the North of Scotland, Orkney and Shetland Shipping Company stores. The company served Orkney and Shetland from Aberdeen and Leith under varying titles for almost a century becoming part of P&O Ferries in 1970. These extensions were demolished at the renovations creating a wider effect to the pier. The pier was extended in a northerly and then easterly direction to create the current appearance. Along the Ayre Road the whiteness of the Ayre Hotel stands out, and many other old familiar features can also be spotted. On Harbour Street the whiteness of "The North of Scotland" office is also prominent. This is now the office of Graham Sutherland, solicitor.

• c.1955 •

For many years swimming facilities in Kirkwall —
indeed in Orkney itself — were confined to the open sea.
In Kirkwall there had been a swimming club long before
the war. Swimming was either at Scapa or in Kirkwall
Harbour, "the Basin," the latter not always the cleanest
or clearest of places with oil from ships and other
detritus. Pictured here at the steps at the north east
corner of the Basin are back row, Jimmie Learmonth,
Mike Parkins, Jack Rendall, John Mowat and Colin
Wooldrage while in the front are Alan Kelday, Tommy
Bews, Armit Leslie, George Harrison and Norman Muir.

• c.1971 •

These old houses within the shadow of the "Moosie Tour" of the Bishops' Palace in Palace Road dated back far into Kirkwall's history. In the 17th century the houses were described as the "ludgeing or long tenement," and at the beginning of the nineteenth century (1823) came into the hands of Hay Elrick, a watchmaker, who purchased them from the descendants of William Orem, Notary Public and Town Clerk of Kirkwall (died 1703). The houses comprised 3-9 Palace Road (which until c.1910 was called Palace Street) and in 1900 housed ten tenants.

• c.1971 •

This picture shows the Palace Road houses being demolished to create the present houses on the site. The large house with its gable end facing up Palace Road was erected by Hay Elrick in front of the western end of the "ludgeing." This house, which was 1 Palace Road, had a dental surgery in part of it in the 1920s. Its front door, which is no longer in existence, opened on to Palace Road.

• Mid-1960s •

This view of the east end of Shore Street shows the roof of No 26 being stripped, presumably in preparation for demolition because the house was removed to create further changes at the junction with St Catherine's Place from which the county library van can be seen emerging. Previous demolition of a wall at this corner had already widened the junction. Today the area is even more greatly changed with a roundabout at the spot where the lorry is about to turn right. A close went from where the "Road Closed" sign is and allowed access to St Catherine's Place at what was formerly Erskine Square.

• c.1962 •

St Catherine's Place. This photograph of the north end shows the demolition work in progress on the wall and other buildings to widen the access from Shore Street.

• c.1960s •

St Catherine's Place looking north. This view reminds us of the narrowness of this end of the road. In this narrow section of the road stood Jolly's coal stores and the North of Scotland Shipping Company's cattle sheds. On the left beyond the waterpump is the entrance to what was Erskine Square. At the extreme left is Cox's shop. The waterpump was a common feature at corners of the town. This was where the populace could draw water before internal water supplies existed.

• Early 1970s •

Kirkwall East Side. This aerial view probably taken in the early 1970s has some features which have been altered, especially in the 1990s. On the Shore Street sea front and stretching along the shingle and cliff to Cromwell Road, massive land reclamation led to the building of a car park, a roundabout at the St Catherine's Place junction and the extension of Shore Street to link with Cromwell Road just at the left edge of the picture. The area along Shore Street from the bottom edge of the picture and across the St Catherine's Place junction is the oldest part of the town where the first dwellings were established before the 9th century. The length of Cromwell Road from the corner with the block of five houses, centre left, facing the shore was formerly called Young Street and the area of land between it and the

shore where S. & J. D. Robertson's offices and the new ambulance station stand was popularly known from the 17th century as "Dunkirk." At the end of Shore Street is the slipway leading on to the shore itself. On the right to the rear of what was R. Garden's and more recently Scarthcentre can be seen the small round peaked building known as the "Groattie House." Sometimes called "Gow's Folly" it was built as a summer-house by James Traill, provost of Kirkwall in 1730. In the top left can be seen the Portacabin workshop of "Ortak Jewellery" which was begun by Malcolm Gray in his shed at Buttquoy Drive in 1967. As the business developed it moved to his brother Maurice's garage in Mount Drive around 1970 and the Portacabin was later added for more space.

• 1979 •

Music always played a large part in Dougie Shearer's life. This photograph was taken at the launch of a new LP *Music from The Orkney Isles* in May 1979. The picture features in the back row the American Nancy Cassell, Billy and Ingrid Jolly, and in front Allie Windwick and Hugh Inkster. Nancy Cassell had spent some years in Orkney collecting local music and songs. Side one of the LP was a tribute to Allie Windwick who wrote many Orkney songs while side two featured Nancy on guitar accompanying Hugh on the fiddle with a variety of tunes both local and national.

• 1980 •

Kirkwall Amateur Operatic Society Orchestra. This shows one half of the orchestra rehearsing for *The Gondoliers* the production of that year. The orchestra was first formed for a production of the pantomime *Cinderella* in 1921 under the name Kirkwall Amateur Orchestra. After the formation of the operatic society which first performed with *The Mikado* in 1925 the orchestra became associated with it and in the years since has played the music at most of the society's productions. The orchestra was another interest of Dougie Shearer who played in it. Seen here are: back row, Jack Ridgway, Jim Robertson, Alex Bain; row two, Lib Shearer, Heather Moodie, Jane Versteeg, Katherine Donaldson, Hugh Black; row three, Alan Gifford, Lesley Macleod, Elaine Grieve; front row, Leslie Tait, Ian McKune, Elma Marshall, John Laughton.

• 1980 •

This shows the other half of the orchestra under its conductor Ed Holt. The musicians are David Leslie (standing at the back), row two, Mark Rendall, Sheelagh Prendergast, Peter Saunders; front, John Laughton, Libby Kelsall, Helen Shearer, Louis Newell. Also at the back almost hidden by the piano is Rosemary Burgon.

• c.1980 •

KGS Oboe Quintet. From 1972-88 Dougie was a music instructor with Orkney Islands Council education department. Dougie played strings but was also keen on the saxophone thus had a keen interest in the instruments here. The quintet played quite often. This picture shows Graham Walker at the back, with Ian Tait, Peter Marshall, David Leslie and Andrew Walker in the front.

• 1965 •

This photograph was taken on board *St Ola* to provide the cover for the record *Owre the Ferry* recorded by Angus Findlater accompanied by Alex Windwick, nephew of Allie Windwick who composed the title song. Side one featured *Owre the Ferry* and *Sleepie Laddie*, while side two contained *Lonely Scapa Flow* and *Isie's Gan tae Brew*. *Lonely Scapa Flow* was very evocative recalling the war era when the Flow was the base for Britain's Home Fleet and was a hive of activity, but in post-war years after the base closed became again a quiet, deserted place. The record was produced by Phoenix Records another of Dougie's Shearer's interests.

• c.Early 1980's •

In 1977 the composer Peter Maxwell-Davies along with Orkney's poet and writer George Mackay Brown launched the St Magnus Festival, a programme of musical concerts and recitals, poetry recitals etc. Orkney's schools' musicians took part along with guest orchestras, quartets etc. from the UK mainland. This shows Kirkwall Schools under teacher and conductor Dick Hughes practising for a performance. Back row, Aimee Robertson, ?, Ingrid Donaldson, Margaret Thomson; row two, Alice Kelsall, Morraine Sinclair, Erika Jolly, Dinah Burgess, Alison Leonard, Ruth Johnston, Monica Bremner, Tracy Muir, Lyndsey Irvine, Arlene Peace; front, Catherine Thomson, Lynette Harcus, Yvonne Harcus, Fiona Cromarty, Rob Walker, Richard Flett, David Rendall.

• c.Early 1980's •

Schools Orchestra. Another view of the orchestra practising for a performance for the St Magnus Festival. Back row, Ingrid Donaldson, Margaret Thomson; row two, Mrs Glynis Hughes, Alice Kelsall, Marraine Sinclair, Erika Jolly, Dinah Burgess, Ruth Johnston, Tracy Muir, Arlene Peace, Lyndsey Irvine, ? Front; Catherine Thomson, Lynnette Harcus, Yvonne Harcus, Fiona Cromarty, Rob Walker, Richard Flett.

During World War II Italian prisoners captured in North Africa by British forces were sent to UK for internment for the remainder of the war. In January 1942 six hundred Italian POWs were brought to Orkney to assist Balfour Beatty's workforce in completing the construction of the Churchill Barriers. This was ostensibly 'war-work' but the possible contravening of Geneva Regulations was overcome by detailing it as a civilian work to link the southern islands to Orkney's mainland for better access for the locals.

Two camps were established — Camp 60 on Lambholm and Camp 34 on Burray. In Camp 60 was an artist called Domenico Chiocchetti who firstly constructed a statue in the camp 'square' of St George slaying the dragon. When it was proposed to build a Chapel the authorities gave it their blessing. A Nissen hut became the prisoners' chapel. Chiocchetti sculpted the chapel and painted it. Another prisoner made the rood-screen from iron provided by Balfour Beatty and another made the brass candlesticks. The chapel was also lit by electricity which added to the effect.

After the war, the chapel fell into disrepair over the years. In 1960 Chiocchetti who had been traced to his home in Italy came back to restore it and a re-dedication ceremony took place in April 1960. Signor Chiocchetti returned for a final visit in 1963. He died in 1999 aged 88.

• Early 1970s •

Stanger Head, Flotta. In 1970 oil was discovered in the British sector of the North Sea. After much deliberation as to where to bring the oil from the Piper Field ashore it was decided that Flotta was strategically the ideal site. Though the oil terminal was eventually to be on the Golta peninsula at the north end of the island this picture of Stanger Head in the south of the island with the remains of the war-time look-out tower reminds us of another period when Flotta's strategical siting made it of prime importance in the defence of Scapa Flow. Indeed, as this book is published there are plans being laid for the island to become an international container hub.

• c.1975 •

In September 1973 Orkney Islands Council gave outline planning permission for the building of the oil terminal at Flotta. Formal planning permission was granted in January 1974 and within weeks work to construct the terminal was under way. These pictures show the work in progress and the workers' camp site.

• c.1975 •

• 1977 •

The arrival of oil brought a new boost to Orkney's traditional agricultural economy which twice before in the twentieth century had received outside fillips, but rather more sadly from the advent of the World Wars. The first oil came ashore in December 1976. This picture was taken at the official opening of the terminal on 11th January 1977 when Britain's Energy Minister, Tony Benn (front left) pulled a lever to mark the start of production.

Alongside him is Flotta resident Tom Rosie (aged 92) who received a cheque for £25,000 on behalf of the community from Occidental towards the new community centre; next is Dr Armand Hammer, head of Occidental Petroleum Corp., operators of the oil field, and next is Piper "Mac" Robertson who composed and played *Flotta Hammer* to pipe the oil ashore.

This picture taken on the day the summer holidays began shows pupils leaving the old Kirkwall Grammar School for the last time. This entrance/exit was once known as the "Girls' Gate," the "Boys' Gate" having been lower down School Place. At the right-hand pillar is the gable end of the building which in the 50s and early 60s housed the library and also the sixth year room, known as "Room Q" and later in the 1960s "Room 34." The window at the left-hand pillar was once that of a Primary classroom, before the school became Secondary only. If one turned left at the door, back-centre, there was a long corridor which formerly led to the Infant Department. Turning right led to the Secondary Department most of which was upstairs. The pillars, iron gate, railings and arch were all removed when the school was converted into the council offices in 1978.

• 1971/72 •

This picture shows pupils at the shop popularly known as the "Rocky Shop." The shop dated back to the end of the 19th century when a Mrs Smith sold hand-made rock there. From 1903-23 it was owned by a Mr and Mrs Drever. At the end of the 1920s it became "Louie Foubisters" and remained so until many years later.

After "Louie" a number of people had the shop including a Mrs MacGillivray. Today the "Rocky Shop" has been re-converted to a dwellinghouse, but for generations of pupils it was a "playtime" mecca with huge queues forming along the pavement. The boy crossing the road is Ronnie Peace from Kirkwall.

• c.1975 •

This picture shows the "Up" and "Down" stairs leading to the Secondary Subjects Departments. Pupils went up the stairs on the right. At a half-landing there was the flight of stairs going left in the picture leading to the Science, Geography, Commercial rooms and, prior to 1953, to the Headmaster's study/office. At the beginning of the 50s the Commercial department moved out to a new room in the Boys' playground and after Mr Leask's retirement the Headmaster's room became an English room for senior classes taken by Mr Stephen. Going right from the landing led to French, Maths, English, Latin, History, Art and Domestic Science rooms. At the bottom of the stairs the door at the extreme left edge became the Rector's study. Previously it had been the janitor's room. Before the provision of the bag racks schoolbags lay in a masse in the corners where the racks were built. The all-glass room changed from being a store to the school office in 1953.

This aerial shot shows a great deal of central Kirkwall, especially the old Grammar School in the centre foreground, on the site it had occupied since 1820, though this building dates from 1874. The school's actual origins go far back and was certainly in existence in 1486 because the charter by which James III created the town as a Royal Burgh refers to the school, ownership of which was transferred to the Magistrats of Kirkwall. It probably began in St Magnus Cathedral as a Sang School where the clergy taught singing and Latin which was then the international language used in Church liturgy and business.

Early records always refer to the school as the "Grammar School" because Latin Grammar was taught there. Prior to 1820 the school had been housed near the junction of Broad Street and Palace Road (a plaque marks the site) and from 1764 near the present War Memorial on Broad Street.

In 1818 Samuel Laing offered a corner of his Papdale estates for a new school building which was occupied by 1820. At the same time a new Subscription School (teaching English) was established and shared the accommodation. In 1833 due to the efforts of the Rev Dr Paterson an Infant School was built next to the Grammar School. In 1974 a new school was built on the site of these three schools and became known as the Burgh School, the name it was known as until 1931 when it again became Kirkwall Grammar School.

Extensions were built in 1890, 1904, and 1914 when a second storey was added. At the end of the 1940s a concrete building housing two Primary rooms and a Commercial room was erected in the Boys' playground, while in the 1950s a wooden building for two Primary rooms was put up in the front playground on King Street.

All of these features can clearly be seen in the picture as also the main playgrounds and the entrances/exits, including the back gate from the Boys' playground which allowed access to Mill Street. At the bottom end of this playground were the shelters and toilets. Access from the front playground at the corner of School Place and King Street to the small front area at the bell tower was once prevented by railings. The quadrangular area at what was the Infant rooms can also be picked out.

In 1975 the school moved to its present site and the building here became the council offices and many changes occurred.

There are many other features worth noting here too. There is the Paterson Church in the bottom right-hand corner, now the East Kirk. There has been a kirk on this site since 1796. This is to be sold and changes are to be made. The King Street Church can also be seen, as can the present Orkney Library in Laing Street. There is also the old Scout Hall in Mill Street and Leitch's gardens (now Glue's garden centre).

• 1971 •

This picture taken in the Boys' playground shows the Grammar School staff for 1970/71 taken just before the summer holidays. Mr McInnes became head of the Primary School. Tragically Mr MacKerron, the rector, died during the holidays. The window in the right hand corner was a cloakroom window while the other two ground floor windows were of the Woodwork room which later became the Metalwork room. Back row, Maurice Manson, Michael Drever, Donald Mainland, Harold Esson, Jack Omand, Liam Stewart, Donald MacInnes, Stewart Norquoy, Louis Newell, Frank Turner, Clive Strutt, Edgar Gibson, John MacDonald, Sandy Wylie, Jimmie Dearness; row two, Fred Rose, Lister Hogarth, George Blance, Sandy Firth, Magnus Ritch, Ray Fereday, Helen Donaldson, Mary Thomson, Avril McCann, Jean Mitchell, Willie Buchan, Norman Mitchell, Ed Headley, Ian Milne, Jack Adam; seated, Elizabeth Hall, Ethel Twatt, John Macallum, Susan Flint, Dan Rosie, Brenda Mowat, Alex Stephen, Harry MacKerron (Rector), Annie Laird, Jimmie Dewar, Jean Work, Evelyn Stockan, George Scott, Kathleen Twatt, Mary Bain and Frances Mitchell.

• c.1975 •

This is a classroom in the old Grammer School. From the maps on the wall and the details on the blackboard it seems to be either a History or Modern Studies room. Note the desks and the fire. Previously there was an open coal fire with a guard rail (the eye-hooks can still be seen) and it was a favourite ploy of the boys in particular on a winter's day to spend lengthy periods at the fire sharpening and re-sharpening pencils which seemed to break frequently. This may have been a former Primary classroom next to the bell tower or an upstairs room. The absence of a partition at the right-hand side makes it difficult to pinpoint the location. This was the only room where the clock did not have a pediment above it.

Another classroom in the old Grammar School showing the double desks and the partition separating the room from the next classroom. This room was downstairs and was probably Room 7 or 8 to judge from the size of the desks. Its windows at the back overlook the lane from the Girls' Gate to the main entrance. Note the ventilator in the back corner.

• c.1972 •

This was the old woodwork room which became a metalwork room. The pupils have new aprons, and there is new shelving beside the window to carry steel stock. There is a swinging ladder from the shelving. All these features were the initiative of the teacher Sandy Firth. The shelving was made from "handy-angle" from James Flett & Sons. Just below the window is a domestic cooker adapted for plastic dip-coating.

• 1970s •

Orkney's Education Committee around the time of local government reorganisation. Standing, Frank Kent, Jack Scott, Jackie Groat, George Marwick, George Marshall (depute director), Reg Dixon (finance dept), John Scott, Brenda Robertson, Nigel Firth, Margaret Porteous, Jackie Tait, Roger Robson (administration officer), Jim Robertson (teacher rep). Seated, Susie Gilbertson (teacher rep), Laura Grimond, Christine Muir, Ewan Traill, George Stevenson, Alex Bain (director).

• 1978 •

Adventure Playground, Papdale Primary School. The playground was constructed from drainage pipes and was the idea of John MacDonald principal P.E. teacher. The item here is meant to be a ship. In the right corner is "the hill." There was also a train shape. Eventually they were dismantled because they were considered a safety risk. The playground is now the site of the link block between the Infant and Primary Schools. Amongst the pupils seen here in the foreground are Wayne Newlands, Stuart Heddle, Kirsten Mears, Philip Malcolm and Derek Sutherland.

• 1976 •

Papdale Primary School Staff. The first phase of the Papdale School's campus began in the 1950s when the Infant School was opened in 1955 and this picture is taken outside it. The Primary School opened in 1962. Recently at the very end of the 20th century a new block linking the two schools was completed. The 1976 staff featured are: back row, Margaret Gray, Willie Harper, Ann McKemmie, Patsy Dickinson, Moira Eunson, Hilda Walls, Caroline Nixon, Elaine Urquhart, Leslie Manson; row two, Grace Donaldson, Davina Leask, Marjory Heddle, Caroline Drever, Sheena Drever, Jane Versteeg, Ann Sinclair, Tina Leslie, Jean McKinlay, Linda Ramsay, Sally Hayday, Anita Grieve, Jack Cromarty; row three, Philip Stout, Sheelagh Prendergast, Dorothy Thomson, Joyce Moore, Muriel Wylie, Emilie Kirkness, Elma Bews, Ethel Young, Wilma Taylor, Rhoda Corsie, Dave Grieve, Ronnie Allan; front row, Elma Marshall, Sheila Allen, Inga Oag, Margo Kemp, Isobel Drever, Donald McInnes, Barbara Vescoe, Bertha Fiddler, Rev. Bill Cant, Susie Gilbertson, Fiona Bain.

• c.1974 •

New Kirkwall Grammar School. This shows the almost completed secondary school complex which was first fully occupied in August 1975. The playing fields are in use, and the Primary School pitches are in the bottom left. Meadowbank housing scheme, in the bottom right, is also almost completed, being occupied by 1975. Since then the Papdale private housing scheme has been built though the link road, now known as The Meadows can be seen. The school has also had a front car park and new office extension built between itself and the link road.

• c.1971 •

This photograph probably taken about 1971 shows the first phase of the new Grammar School complex — the swimming pool and games hall — in course of construction. Towards the bottom left is part of the Papdale Primary School. On the north side of Berstane Road a good number of the houses seen in the 1974 picture have still not been constructed.

• Early 1970s •

East Road leading to the farm of Waterfield in the top centre, passing Eastbank Hospital and the first private houses built in the Easthill quarries area. Eastbank Hospital, formerly the old family home of Eastbank House, dating from late 19th century, was first used as a fever hospital and for TB patients in 1937, replacing the one which had been at Scapa. Latterly it became a hospital for geriatric and other incapacitated patients before closing in the late 1990s.

• c.1968 •

Albert Street showing the "Big Tree" and other established features of the era. The tree was once formerly in a garden and dates back some three hundred years. For a good number of years it had an iron railing around it. The family butcher James McDonald dated from 1927. In the late 1970s it became Christine Clarke's Antiques. The Tree Bakery was established in 1934 by D. & L. Nicolson in the premises of Sclater Brothers, and is now The Tree Shop. Swanson's Hair Stylist dated from 1924 and became Hazel's Hairstylist in the 1980s though Hazel had traded there since 1972. Above McDonald's sign is the window of the room where Orkney's first telephone exchange was opened in September 1923. Orkney was the last county in Scotland to get an exchange, and it remained in these premises until 1952/53 when it removed to Palace Road which is shown in our other picture and which was then in use until the most recent one was built alongside it.

• 1968 •

• Late 1960's •

The Longship. Ola Tait (neé Gorie) is now internationally known for her jewellery, but this picture shows Ola (right) with Jean Tulloch in her shop which then had much more fancy goods, though the showcases at the front are displaying her jewellery. She founded her business in 1960 after graduating from college. Working from a shed in the garden of here parents' house in King Street, Ola produced jewellery in gold and silver – the first locally made jewellery since Norse times. Her designs were the Maeshowe Dragon, the Papa Stronsay Cross, and a design from the Cathedral.

After her marriage in 1961 she moved to Canada for a few years, but the business was kept running by her mother. After her return she bought Bill Brough's shop in Broad Street. It had space at the back to build a workshop and expand her business, which has had three extensions since then. In 1999 she was awarded the MBE for her work.

• c.1968 •

This picture shows Reynold Eunson at work carving the figure of a soldier watched by Stanley Cursiter, the distinguished Orcadian artist who was keeper of the National Galleries of Scotland 1930-48 and Painter and Limner to the Queen until his death in 1976, aged 89. He and Reynold Eunson collaborated closely in the creation and design of the St Rognvald Chapel in St Magnus Cathedral.

• c.1968 •

This shows Reynold Eunson at work on the carving of Kol, father of St Rognvald, the builder of St Magnus Cathedral. Reynold Eunson also carved statues of Rognvald and of Bishop William the Old, the first bishop of the Cathedral.

In addition the communion table and chairs for the minister and elders were also carved by Reynold, a well-known maker of the traditional straw-backed Orkney chairs. He died at the early age of 46 in 1978.

• c.1973 •

This shows the hull of a fibreglass boat being constructed in Halmatic's factory in one of the old World War II hangars at Hatston. Halmatic, a firm from Havant in Hampshire, produced their first hull in November 1971. The factory cost £25,000. The boats were a success, but in 1977, following the fishing recession, the workforce dropped from 50 to 12. The firm was rescued through a joint effort by Orkney Islands Council and the Highlands & Islands Development Board in May 1977. The firm now extended their work to constructing whole boats themselves. In January 1979 there was a huge response from the Boat Show, but by July trade difficulties aggravated by world-wide conditions forced the firm to close. In its eight years it produced around 84 craft, including 36 footers (47), 29ers (16), 24 footers (6), 54 footers (6) and five of the Highland Admiral Class.

• c.1970 •

The "Herald Bookshop" was once the front shop for *The Orkney Herald* the other local weekly newspaper published from 17th April 1860 until 10th January 1961. Its first editor was James Tait with Wm Peace as secretary & treasurer. In 1870 Peace became the proprietor. In 1921 George Leonard the bookseller and his brother-in-law James Twatt purchased the business which, in 1935, came under the sole ownership of James Twatt. His son, Jack, was the paper's last editor. At the height of its popularity it had a readership of 5,000, and in addition to news, sport, articles, featured the famous stories of the imaginary parish of Stenwick, the Sooan Sids columns, Cubbie Roo's writings, and Islandman (George Mackay Brown). From 1868-1940 it also published the annual Peace's Almanack. Its print works were down the lane beside it on Junction Road. The bookshop itself continued until it became Robert Learmonth's in the 1970s, before becoming A.J.B. Scholes accountants in the 1980s.

• 1982 •

Some of *The Orcadian* (est. 1854) printing staff checking (or having read of) the news in the latest edition as it rolls off the press on the 10th March in its Victoria Street premises. An interesting feature here is that the paper was still broadsheet with news on the front page. Front page news had been carried by the paper from December 1908 until March 1916 when newprint shortages forced the size of the paper to be reduced with advertisements on the front. In 1966, after half a century, the paper reverted to front page news again. In 1988 the paper became tabloid-size. Another interesting item is the Cossar printing press which is now on display in the reception of the firm's Hatston premises where production staff re-located in 1996. The staff pictured are Kenny Thomson, Davie Oag, Adrian Harray and Fred Grieve.

• 1972 •

On Friday March 17th the printworks of *The Orcadian* were destroyed by fire, the worst calamity to strike the paper in its 118 years of existence. Firemen fought the blaze for five hours. A human chain of staff and neighbours in the darkness of the night and the choking fumes helped to save valuable records including all the past files of the *The Orcadian*, which were transferred to the Royal Bank of Scotland nearby. Despite the fire the paper continued to be published as usual without break on Thursdays thanks to the newspaper press at the back being saved and to help from newspapers in Wick and Shetland. Within six months a temporary premises was constructed allowing a resumption of all printing services.

This was the old woodwork room which became a
metalwork room. The pupils have new aprons, and there
is new shelving beside the window to carry steel stock.
There is a swinging ladder from the shelving. All these
features were the initiative of the teacher Sandy Firth.
The shelving was made from "handy-angle" from James
Flett & Sons. Just below the window is a domestic
cooker adapted for plastic dip-coating.

• 1968 •

Cosmo Ballroom, Kirkwall. The ballroom had been started in 1947 by D. B. Peace & Co who had once had Orkney's first cinema in this building. For at least a quarter of a century the "Coser" reverberated to the beat of the music and the dancing feet of its patrons. The occasion shown here was a special function to promote a film about Orkney's bank boat "The *OtterBank*." The band who played at this function was the "Alphabeats" featuring Robert Swanney (guitar), Alan Keldie (guitar), Brian Peace (sax), Robert Milne (organ) and Jim

("Mosh") Marwick on drums. The gentleman in the suit and pullover walking down the left hand side of the hall is Jim Sinclair, now of the Mills petrol station, who also features in the close-up photo in the foreground with his back to the camera talking to his sister Isobel (on his right). Others include Ian Gibson, Ida Cromarty and possibly Alistair Yule. Others in the over-view include Marcus Liddle who ran the Orphir Youth Club before going to central Scotland as a Youth Officer, Edric Clouston and Jim Mainland.

• 1968 •

• 1976 •

Papdale Primary School Staff. The first phase of the Papdale School's campus began in the 1950s when the Infant School was opened in 1955 and this picture is taken outside it. The Primary School opened in 1962. Recently at the very end of the 20th century a new block linking the two schools was completed. The 1976 staff featured are: back row, Margaret Gray, Willie Harper, Ann McKemmie, Patsy Dickinson, Moira Eunson, Hilda Walls, Caroline Nixon, Elaine Urquhart, Leslie Manson; row two, Grace Donaldson, Davina Leask, Marjory Heddle, Caroline Drever, Sheena Drever, Jane Versteeg, Ann Sinclair, Tina Leslie, Jean McKinlay, Linda Ramsay, Sally Hayday, Anita Grieve, Jack Cromarty; row three, Philip Stout, Sheelagh Prendergast, Dorothy Thomson, Joyce Moore, Muriel Wylie, Emilie Kirkness, Elma Bews, Ethel Young, Wilma Taylor, Rhoda Corsie, Dave Grieve, Ronnie Allan; front row, Elma Marshall, Sheila Allen, Inga Oag, Margo Kemp, Isobel Drever, Donald McInnes, Barbara Vescoe, Bertha Fiddler, Rev. Bill Cant, Susie Gilbertson, Fiona Bain.

• c.1974 •

New Kirkwall Grammar School. This shows the almost completed secondary school complex which was first fully occupied in August 1975. The playing fields are in use, and the Primary School pitches are in the bottom left. Meadowbank housing scheme, in the bottom right, is also almost completed, being occupied by 1975. Since then the Papdale private housing scheme has been built though the link road, now known as The Meadows can be seen. The school has also had a front car park and new office extension built between itself and the link road.

• 1971 •

Orkney Territorial Army. This picture shows members of the Orkney detachment TA prior to departure on an RAF Andover on the 11th June for a weekend exercise in infantry support weapons at Otterburn, Northumberland. These men were following a calling dating back to 1908 when the first TA was set up, though its origins go back to the days of the 19th century volunteer forces. The 1st Orkney Artillery Volunteers are recorded in 1867, and in the next forty years became the Administrative Brigade Orkney Artillery Volunteers, the Orkney Artillery Volunteer Corps and Orkney Royal Garrison Artillery (Volunteers).

Just prior to 1940 there were three detachments in

Kirkwall — 226 Heavy AA Battery TA, which shot down the first German aircraft over British soil, the Orkney Heavy Reg RA. Coastal Defence, and the Orkney Fortress Engineers RE. After the war there was 430 Coast Reg TA, 861 (Indep) LAA Battery RA. (TA) and also at one stage Lovat Scouts. Featured here are Freddie Rorie, Gordon Thomson, Jimmy Leask, Jimmy Craigie, Norn Donaldson, Leslie Plowman, Kenny Chalmers, Willem Schinkel, Davy Linklater, Gordon (?) Chalmers, Abbie Lang, Jim Coutts, Murray Soutter, Dennis Petrie, Willie Sutherland, Brian Park. The officer briefing them is Gary Gibson.

•   1970s   •

Ayre Hotel. The hotel forms the foreground feature of this picture. At the end of the 19th century it was Black's Temperance Hotel. The Ayre Road was built on part of the "Aire" (meaning shore) a stretch of shingle land which ran west from the Kiln Corner to the Ayre Mills (where Mills petrol station is now) and which for centuries separated the open sea to the north from the "Peerie Sea" to the south. Even in 1800 the Peerie Sea covered the area in the picture occupied by Burnmouth Road, Great Western Road, and all the section towards

the top right-hand corner. Since the late 1980s roundabouts have been built at the Kiln Corner (top left) and the Burnmouth/Ayre Roads junction. Burgh Road has been constructed from the bend in Burnmouth Road, south westwards through the burgh yard to Great Western Road. And recently in the top west side of Kiln Corner a new office/residential block has been built. Land reclamation on the shore led to the building of the Shapinsay Ferry Terminal.

• c.1968 •

Albert Street showing the "Big Tree" and other established features of the era. The tree was once formerly in a garden and dates back some three hundred years. For a good number of years it had an iron railing around it. The family butcher James McDonald dated from 1927. In the late 1970s it became Christine Clarke's Antiques. The Tree Bakery was established in 1934 by D. & L. Nicolson in the premises of Sclater Brothers, and is now The Tree Shop. Swanson's Hair Stylist dated from 1924 and became Hazel's Hairstylist in the 1980s though Hazel had traded there since 1972. Above McDonald's sign is the window of the room where Orkney's first telephone exchange was opened in September 1923. Orkney was the last county in Scotland to get an exchange, and it remained in these premises until 1952/53 when it removed to Palace Road which is shown in our other picture and which was then in use until the most recent one was built alongside it.

• Early 1979 •

This picture shows the new Co-op being built on Pickaquoy Road. The Co-op had been present in Kirkwall in Bridge Street since about 1941/42. It opened in these new premises in November 1979. In the bottom right corner is the almost completed Glaitness Primary School which opened earlier in the same year. Close to the Co-op is the council yard and further along in the direction of the town is one of the yards of St Clair's Emporium, now the site of Safeway's supermarket. Also in the picture is the last of Kirkwall's gasometers at the back of the Phoenix Cinema. This gasometer was removed in 1979 and a residential caravan park is now on the site, while the Glaitness Park housing development occupies the fields behind the Emporium yard and the Co-op.

• 1978 •

Junction Road. Quite a number of changes have taken place in this area. The gasometer was removed in 1979 and the residential caravan site is there now. The car park in what was known as "The Crafty" alongside the Phoenix has had the wall reconstructed and extended to be parallel to the cinema. The old slaughterhouse to the right of The Crafty became the new Scout Hall in 1987 and the Multiple Sclerosis Therapy Centre. Across the road from The Crafty two gardens have become a car park and the buildings at the bottom of them removed for the entrance to the car park. The white building with the van alongside it was formerly the Post Office parcel-sorting office and then Scapa Knitwear's premises before being knocked down to make way for the new residential blocks. The tennis courts (part of Costie's) to the left have also been replaced with private houses on the site.

• Early 1950s •

The shell of the Albert Kinema. Judging from the weather-beaten poster advertising *Comanche Territory* - produced 1950 - and the railings this picture dates from the early 1950's. On 8th May 1947 the Albert Kinema which had shown films to the local public since September 1928 was destroyed by fire. Mr John Cooper, storeman at Boots the Chemists next door, raised the alarm, but within 20 minutes the building was ablaze. It took six hours to contain the fire and the local fire brigade was helped by British and Polish soldiers to save adjoining premises. The "Kinema" seated 400 and in April 1939 had shown the world premieré of *The Spy in Black*, a film based on the Orcadian author J. Storer Clouston's tale. The Kinema had formerly been the shop of D. B. Peace, cabinetmaker, who pioneered the cinema in Orkney by opening The Electric Theatre on Junction Road in 1913 on the site of what became the Cosmo ballroom. Following the fire Dougie Shearer, who was cinema manager, announced that films would now be shown in the Temperance Theatre in Mill Street. This was to last until the Phoenix was eventually opened in 1955.

For years the site was derelict. In 1972 Templeton's, who had acquired the nationwide chain of Lipton's, opened a "supermarket" on the site. Templeton's were in turn taken over by Presto's who became Safeway's. Today the premises are occupied by Boots the Chemists, whose site next door was taken over by Gorn Sport.

• 1940s •

This rather grainy picture gives us a rare view of the inside of the Albert Kinema. The little stand in the centre of the foyer lists the films showing and categories: A, "passed for public exhibition to adult audiences"; and U, for "universal audiences".

• c.1966 •

Renovation of the Temperance Hall. This building became the Orkney Arts Theatre and was opened in 1967 after three years of fundraising, providing Orkney with a permanent home for drama, operattas and other entertainment. The first performance was Pitlochry Festival Theatre in *School for Scandal*. The birth of one act plays and the Kirkwall Arts Club dates to 1944 when Donald Hewlitt, (later to achieve fame in television's *It Ain't Half Hot Mum*) was stationed in Orkney with the forces. The hall itself dated from 1823 as the first building for the Congregational Kirk and from 1876 as the meeting place for the Order of Good Templars until 1940. The Good Templars were founded in Utica, New York in 1851 in a period of social reform with the object of having education in temperance in, and abstinence from, the use of intoxicating liquor. During the war it served as the Naval cinema.

• Early 1950s •

The interior of the Temperance Hall showing the projection room used when it was the Navy cinema in the war and then by D. B. Peace from 1947-55. During those eight years it was a popular place for children's matinees on Saturday afternoons with the main feature and serials such as *Flash Gordon*.

• c.1957 •

On the 14th June, 1955 the Phoenix Cinama opened to replace the Albert Kinema, destroyed by fire in 1947. It was opened by Provost James Flett and was described as being one of the finest cinemas in the country for a town of comparable size to Kirkwall. The first film was *Doctor in the House*. Admission prices were Balcony 2/6 (13p) or reserved 3/- (15p) Stalls 2/- (10p) and Front Stalls 1/6 (8p). 14 and under 14 got in for 1/- front stalls and 1/6 other stalls excluding the balcony. At matinees the price was 9d (4p). The cinema often showed special films and on the occasion of this picture had been showing a film about life in Orkney. Pictured here are D.B. Peace (owner of the cinema and Dougie Shearer's uncle), P. Sutherland Graeme (Lord Lieutenant), ?, Stanley Cursiter, Jim Turfus, Douglas Wood (County Clerk), Tommy Shearer, Alex Doloughan and R.L. Johnson.

• 1982 •

Presto's Refurbishment. This shows the staff of the firm's Kirkwall branch just after the Albert Street store had been refurbished internally in 1982: Lorraine Sutherland, Kay Peace, Pat Brass, Yvonne Langskill, Alistair Hine, Ian Learmonth, John Bremner, Peter MacDuff, Jim Macrae, Fiona Norquoy, Stuart Ross, Margaret Meek, Nan Macrae, ?, Lynn Adams, Jean Craigie, Colin Greig, Johnny Omand, Bill Robson, Graham Rosie, George Brown. The un-named lady was a supervisor who came from Paisley for the opening day.

• 1971 •

Orkney County Select. Inter-county matches have been played against Shetland for the Milne Cup since 1908 and Caithness for the Archer Shield since 1935. This picture taken in 1971, shows a select of ex-county players (with the club they were most associated with) who came out of retirement to play against an ex-Hotspurs select to celebrate Hotspurs Golden Jubilee. Back row, Alistair Muir (Hotspurs), Davie Wylie (Thorfinn), Russell Groundwater (Rovers); middle row, Robbie Pottinger (St Andrews), Arnold Rendall (Rovers), Freddie Hutchison, Bobby Hutchison (both Dounby), Charlie Clouston (Stromness), Jock Cursiter (Rovers), Jim Bews (referee); front row, Dave Tinch, John MacDonald (both Rovers), John Donaldson, Jim Donaldson, Ronnie Muir, Eddie Craigie (all Thorfinn). The County team won 7-3.

• 1971 •

Kirkwall Hotspurs 50th Anniversary. In 1921 a third football team was formed in Kirkwall. It took the name Hotspur after the London club Tottenham Hotspur, who had won the FA Cup that year, and the division two championship in 1919/20. In 1971 they staged an anniversary match to mark their jubilee and this picture shows the ex-players select who came out of retirement to play. Quite a number of the players had also played for other clubs in their careers, (indicated in brackets). The club were very successful in local football in the 1920s and '30s, winning leagues and cups. They had a successful junior team after the war, but ironically in 1971 they had no junior side, while the senior side were playing in Division B. In the '90s they again became very successful in winning Orkney's football trophies.

Pictured are: back row, John Byers, Andy Sinclair, Norman Reid, Clarence Baikie; middle row, Edmund Reid, Cecil Sinclair (Thorfinn), George Stout (Thorfinn), Jimmie Leonard, Bill Sim (Thorfinn), Bob Munro (Thorfinn), Philip Stout (Thorfinn), John Moodie, Vincent Linklater, Jim Bews. Front, Jim Baikie, Jim Crisp, Dougie Wylie, Jackie Miller, Ronald Kemp, Jimmie Sinclair. The Stout brothers, Sim, Munro, Crisp and N. Reid all played senior county, while C. Sinclair, A. Sinclair, and Byers all played junior county.

• 1985 •

Orkney's Islands' Games Squad. In the 1980s the offshore island communities got together to hold an Islands' "Olympic" style games, the first of which was held in 1985 in the Isle of Man. The games are held every two years. Back row, Stan Headley, Ray Slater, Stuart Gray, Melvyn Wick, Graham Wylie, John Scott, Steve Harvey; row two, Nigel Reid, Marina Poke, Karen Sutherland, Kitty Work, Ivan Taylor, Lynn Moar, Marie Wylie, Alan Clouston; row three, Gordon Wilson, Lilian Low, Karen Hogley, Linda Low, Hilary Donaldson, Jenny Leslie, Thorfinn Leslie, Malcolm Corsie, Andrew Crossley, Paul Eggeling; front row, Fiona Mackie, Morven MacKenzie, Caroline Budge, Lorraine Gilmour, Glynis Littlejohn, Adrian Pottinger, Mark Irving, Kevin Hancock.

• c.1980 •

Stromness. The burgh of Stromness has a long association with the sea. For centuries passing ships sought shelter in "Hamnavoe," the sheltered bay which is seen to advantage here. The 18th century wars between Britain and France, the Hudson Bay ships picking up recruits and the whaling ships heading for Greenland were the making of the town. The many small piers are a reminder that formerly Stromness carried out its trade by sea, with no regard to land transport. The main pier in the foreground is the *Pole Star* pier where the Commissioners for Northern Lighthouses' vessel was based. The base dated from 1892 with the first *Pole Star*. Behind the next pier can be seen the old Warehouse pier where the Pentland Firth ferry *St Ola* used to berth. The current Ro-Ro terminal used from 1975 is also prominent. Other features include the white house on its own to the left where the local participants in the Mutiny on the *Bounty* lived, the old Stromness Academy, the North Kirk Manse next to it, and along Cairston Road (top right) the site of the egg-packing station where Richardson's boat-builders are now.

Early 1960s — Stromness North End. Here we see the
Stromness Auction Mart pens in the foreground and the
area of wasteground along the shore which has been
reclaimed to create Ferry Road and the access to the Ro-
Ro terminal in the 1970s. It would appear to be July as
the *St Ola* is dressed overall with flags, and the
fairground stalls can be seen where they used to pitch at
that time for "Shopping Week." The *Ola* pictured is the
second of the name, coming on route in 1951 to replace
the "old" *Ola* which plied the route to Scrabster for 59
years and berthed at the Warehouse pier. The "Mail"
ferry to Scrabster dates from 1856. Beyond this pier is
the South Pier at which a naval vessel, possibly a
minesweeper, is berthed. Beyond the *Pole Star* pier in
the distance is the South End and the Ness where at the
end of the 19th century wooden letties were erected for
the herring fishing when hundreds of vessels crowded
the harbour.

Stromness Centre. This view has a number of interesting features as well as showing the many small piers to advantage. From the bottom right proceeding south (left) there is the Harbour Master's Office with the clock and then the pier where the arts gallery is now centred. This was once where Shearer's had their stores. The next pier has the Nautical School and the white house immediately beyond that is the famous Orcadian artist Stanley Cursiter's house. On the next pier quite a number of figures are gathered. The nearest church is the North Church, which eventually was used by Stromness Academy and is now used as a town hall. The other church is Victoria Street Church, Stromness' parish kirk. In the top right is St Peter's Eventide Home.

• c.1968 •

Kirkwall Harbour. This view shows the *Earl Sigurd* moored in the inner harbour — "the Basin" — as close to the Kirkwall Hotel as it is possible to be. The ship served the North Isles from 1930 until she was replaced by the *Islander* in 1969. The *Sigurd* itself had replaced the *Orcadia* (II) which had been in service for 68 years. In the foreground is the *Otterbank* which for seven years from 1962 served the islands as a floating bank for the National Commercial Bank. The accountant was Willie Groat. In 1969 the National Commercial and Royal Bank of Scotland merged to become the Royal Bank. Across from the Kirkwall Hotel at the corner of Bridge Street is Crawford's coffee and sweet-shop, now Focus on Orkney photographic shop.

• 1960s •

This shows James Watson, bank teller and Davie Irvine, skipper of the *Otterbank* at lunch on board the vessel while out on banking services in the islands.

• c.1978 •

Building the new crane garage on Kirkwall Pier. Note the Harbour Master's office and the weighbridge for goods vehicles. There have been a number of changes here. The office is still there but the weighbridge is now at a new office built on reclaimed land to the rear (east). Adjoining the office on the east and parallel to Shore Street are the new premises of Orkney Ferries. There have been changes too at the corner of the inner harbour. There is a pavement where the cars are parked. The white stanchions are more formidable and are black while the wires have been turned into substantial railings. The stanchions at the office have also been removed.

• Early 1960s •

The inner harbour taken at a flood tide. The ships featured here are the *Shapinsay* which carried eggs from Orkney to Glasgow via the Caledonian Canal during the peak period of egg production. The egg-boxes can be seen on her deck. Lying at the cross-berth is the *Orkney Dawn*.

The Corn Slip has its usual complement of youngsters fishing for sillocks off it. The name Corn Slip refers to the time when grain rentals were landed here. In the

background are the offices and sheds of what was once Cooper's who operated the *Amelia*, a cargo vessel trading with Leith. Again many changes have taken place in the area. There are two high storage tanks on the site of the Amelia offices and store. The nissen huts on the main pier have been demolished. There is a pavement along the harbour edge and the stanchions are more substantial.

• Early 1950s •

Early 1950s — Another view of Kirkwall Harbour taken in snowtime. In the background is the *St Ninian* one of the ships of the North of Scotland, Orkney and Shetland Shipping Co. which plied between Leith, Aberdeen, Kirkwall and Lerwick. At the west side is the Orkney Steam Navigation Co.'s *Earl Sigurd*. The *Orkney Trader* lies at the main pier, while the *Shapinsay* is at the cross-berth. On the pier are the gas-lamps which were converted to electricity and the black and white stripes painted on in war-time to help vehicles avoid them in black-out can still be seen. Numerous changes have occurred here. The pier at the "Basin" has been widened as has the main pier for the "North" boats, which has been greatly lengthened, widened and extended in a northern and then eastern direction to allow cruise liners to dock alongside instead of anchoring in the bay, though the largest still do. The corner of the West pier at the exit from the "Basin" has also been widened in a circular manner and the steps in the corner are no longer there. The light which once stood at the north point of the pier was removed to this part of the West Pier at the time of the renovations. The "North" sheds at the point had lean-to sections on both sides which were removed, in effect widening the pier. The sheds themselves were converted to offices for P&O Ferries.

• c.1968 •

This aerial view shows in the right foreground the second phase of the Quoybanks housing scheme in the course of construction. The first houses in Craigie Crescent have been completed. In the centre is the old Cathedral manse from which Manse Road took its name when the scheme incorporating it, Laverock Road, Broadsands Road, etc was built in the late 1940s. The playpark at the rear of the council houses in the Clay Loan also stands out. The Cathedral manse is now flats. Note the extent of the Peerie Sea and the area round it before all the changes there.

• Late 1960s •

Kirkwall West Side. There are many features here where changes have occurred. The Hydro station on the shore of the Peerie Sea has built an extension towards the car park at "Picky" Road. The picture must have been taken in July/August since the fairground or 'market' with sideshows etc is there at the roadside. Along "Picky" road is the St Clair's Emporium yards, council yards long before the Co-op, Safeways, Glaitness School were built there or the housing schemes. The Auction Mart sheds between Junction Road and Great Western Road are another prominent feature. With the Mart now at Hatston this site is earmarked for the new County Library. The old power station building from which electricity was supplied 1920-53 can also be seen on Junction Road. In 1972 apporval was given for the Peerie Sea scheme which led eventually to the present facilities and landscaping.

• c.1970 •

Kirkwall School Hostel nearing completion at Papdale. The previous hostel (for girls only) had been in the former Post Office buildings in Old Scapa Road since 1946. Boys requiring lodgings stayed in private houses. Now all isles pupils coming into Kirkwall Grammar School could be under one roof. It was occupied from 1971. The road layout to the hostel has been altered and education houses were constructed to the rear of the houses on Berstane Road in the field stretching towards Papdale Farm in 1975. Further out Berstane Road private houses have been constructed on both sides of the road creating Cursiter Crescent etc. Sheltered by the trees is Papdale House, one of Kirkwall's historic residences, home of the noted historian Malcolm Laing whose father bought the property in 1793. Malcolm was also MP for Orkney 1807-12. He published his *History of Scotland* in 1800.

• c.Mid-1970s •

Corner of High Street and Old Scapa Road. The old houses in the centre of the picture were demolished at the beginning of the 1980s. Both of them dated back to probably at least the beginning of the 19th century and had been occupied by the late Bill Leonard's family for over a century. The house next door in the Scapa direction was Robertson's grocers from 1897 until the 1940s. The old houses were replaced by an extension to this house. The layout of the road was also altered in the 1990s with a wide sweep of pavement being created at this corner.

• c.1977 •

This picture shows Burnarvie House which at one time housed several families at the one time. Today it is empty and is part of W. R. Tullock's car park property. A wall was also erected separating Tullock's parking area from the public car park which stretches in L-shape from Castle Street to Junction Road. Note the Ford Anglia in front of CBS 759L. This was a very popular model from 1959 until it was replaced by the Escort in 1968.

• Pre 1970s •

Buttquoy Place. These old houses were renovated in the 1970s and the garage moved further back from the road. At the beginning of the 20th century Buttquoy Place was part of the road called Back Street which linked Clay Loan with the street now called the Watergate.

• 1979 •

In October this Viscount aircraft operated by Alidair, an
East Midlands' charter company crash landed at
Kirkwall airport at the end of a flight from Glasgow. It
was carrying 47 passengers and four crew and was on a
regular shuttle for the oil company Occidental. The
craft skidded off the main runway and its nose was embedded
in the mud. All on board escaped without injury. The
plane was on loan from Guernsey Airways and carried
their colours. The aircraft was a "write-off" and was
eventually dismantled at Kirkwall.

• 1982 •

Orkney Flying Club with their new plane, a Rallye 150, at Kirkwall Airport. The club was initially an informal one from the late 1940s and one of the early enthusiasts was Sydney Bichan, Orkney's "Flying Farmer" who was still piloting in the late 1980s. In 1954 a Tiger Moth craft was acquired and the club became formal with Ted Gamble as chairman, Bob Learmonth secretary, Bryan Wood, Sydney, and Freddie Pyle as leading lights. Some years later the "Moth" was sold and the club went into abeyance until the early 1970s. By 1973 five members had private pilots licences. The club celebrated its silver jubilee in 1979 with an air show at the airport which was repeated in 1980 and 1982. Pictured here are Brian Findlay, Tommy Sinclair, John Adam, Duncan Peace, Fred Croy, David Steven with his daughter, Pat Sutherland and Andrew Greatrex. In the background is Air Orkney's 'plane.

• Early 1980's •

This picture shows Erling Flett and Duncan Peace, two young Orkney pilots. In 1986 Duncan at the age of 23 became Loganair's youngest captain. He later joined Air 2000 and then Virgin Atlantic. Erling went on to fly with Britannia Airways. In 1999 the two shared a flight deck on London-Johannesburg and London-Tokyo routes.

The Orkney Flying Club managed enough time for a few competitive activities and Duncan is seen here presenting Erling with a trophy. Currently Erling is flying "Jumbos" for Virgin Airways, while Duncan is with Business Air.

• 1981 •

For twenty years Ken Ross and Angus Findlater produced a programme for Radio Orkney called *Oot and Aboot wi' Ken and Angus*. This picture shows them about to set off for Foula on an Air Orkney 'plane piloted by Andy Alsop who set up the airline and chose the Puffin logo. Ken and Angus' programmes were an hour long and the recordings made in Foula covered three transmissions. The signature tune used over the twenty years came from Foula and was recorded on a mandolin and guitar in the Gear family home on the island. The programmes were also broadcast on Radio Scotland. On their way to Foula Andy was interviewed by the duo. Both Ken and Angus have a great sense of humour and can poke fun at themselves as borne out by their tee-shirts with a reference to their "girth." Ken's jersey was red as was Angus' initially though he switched to blue in a very short time. This picture was taken close to the Deerness Road before take-off, showing Ken with recorder, Angus, and Andy.

• 1969 •

The new terminal at Kirkwall Airport. This replaced the old nissen huts which had served from wartime onwards. Grimsetter, as Kirkwall Airport was formerly known, was constructed at the beginning of World War II for the RAF just as Hatston was being completed for the RNAS. Both these airports were part of the large preparation being made for a war which had grown ever nearer. After the war was over it was decided Grimsetter should be Kirkwall's civil airport. In the 1950s the idea of a new terminal building was mentioned but only in 1969 did this occur when it was opened by Jo Grimond MP. This building is about to be replaced by a new terminal which dwarfs this in size.

• 1950s •

This picture shows the old terminal building at Kirkwall Airport. These nissen huts were constructed in 1940 to serve as one of the airfields used in the defence of Orkney and the northern waters. When the war ended, Grimsetter and Hatston were both used as Kirkwall's civil airport, but in 1947 Grimsetter became the county's recognised airport. Curiously not far away, slightly closer to Kirkwall was Wideford which from the inception of flights to Orkney in 1933 until 1939 had been Kirkwall's airport. On entering through the white glass-pannelled door turning to the right took you to the check-in area. Behind the desk at the far end of the area was an office. Turning left brought one to a store and latterly the Customs section. Going on through into the second nissen hut, the end of which is seen on the left, took you to the waiting room and the counter and cooking area. In the centre of this hut was an old fire with its chimney going up through the roof of the hut. The white nissen hut was the fuel hut.

• 1969 •

This picture taken at the opening of the new Kirkwall Airport terminal shows some of BEA's Orkney staff: Jimmy Steen (manager), Harry ('Taffy') Fisher (traffic officer), Donald Macleod (engineer), John Wood (maintenance worker), Brian Kemp (traffic officer), Jack Watson (senior traffic officer).

• 1973 •

In August Katy Devin was born 200 feet above Kirkwall on a Loganair flight from Stronsay to Kirkwall. The flight piloted by Captain Jamie Bayley was trying to land in thick fog when the baby arrived, delivered by Stronsay's GP, Dr G. M. Ferguson, who was accompanying the baby's mother, Mrs Freida Devin, to Kirkwall. The fog forced Captain Bayley to fly on to Aberdeen where mother and baby were admitted to a maternity hospital. Baby Katy was the first baby to be actually born on a Loganair flight and is seen here with her parents Charlie and Freida Devin and Captain Bayley. In 1974 another baby was born in a Loganair flight in Orkney.

This picture shows three Viscount aircraft of BEA (British European Airways) on the apron at Kirkwall Airport. This was an unusual occurence as normally there would be only two. The four-engined, 45-seater Vickers Viscount which flew at 300mph were introduced on the north routes c.1963. The first proving flight of a Viscount had been in May 1956, and the first landing at Kirkwall with passengers was c.December 1962 when many of the passengers were Orkney students returning for Christmas vacation. The Viscount served Orkney until the 1980s and both locally and internationally had a superb safety record.

BEA was formed in 1948 from an amalgamation of several British airlines, including those serving the continent. In the 1970s it merged with BOAC (British Overseas Airways Corporation) to form BA (British Airways).

• 1970 •

These pictures taken c.1970 show the square known as "Spence's Square" in Victoria Street, Kirkwall. The earliest records of the houses here is for one at the north side where the monogram WM can be seen. In the 18th century the property was sold to a Trail family who held it for a century until 1850. It was bought by Peter Shearer, carpenter, builder, carter, undertaker, who extended and renovated the properties. His eldest daughter Mary married the bookseller David Spence and inherited the property, hence Spence's Square. After her death in 1934 family members continued to own it until 1974 when the council obtained it and renovated it.

Spence's Square after renovation. The newly refurbished houses have no ivy on the walls. An iron arch has been erected at the entrance where previously there had been none. The chimney stacks were reduced in height by taking away the brick section which must have been a late 19th century addition. The old stone slates on the roof have been replace by more modern ones (despite being a conservation area) and the skylights have also been removed. A light on the gable end of the southern building was also removed.

• Late 1960s •

The upper end of Victoria Street in the late 1960s. Hidden behind the van is the entrance to Victoria Road. Orkney Television Enterprise whose shop was at the corner of Victoria Street and Victoria Road moved to its Broad Street premises in the late 1960s. Spence's Square on the right underwent complete refurbishment. The wall alongside the van was demolished and is now the entrance to Wm Shearer's Victoria Street garden nursery.

This view of the west side of Victoria Street looking towards its junction with Clay Loan shows principally the old-established (1857) firm of Wm Shearer, grocer, ironmonger, seed merchant before the modernisation of its frontage. The ground floor was extended southerly taking in the lane to 73 Victoria Street and at the same time was moved back westerly thus widening the street and giving the shop a patio area for floral displays etc.

The gable end of the house on the upper stories was demolished. Next door at No. 75 the railings and wall have been removed as has the railings further south in front of what is now the Baptist Church. The property beyond those railings which was once Jocky Sinclair's gents' hairdressers shop and then Donaldson's butcher shop has now been renovated to form flats.

• 1970s •

This view of Mounthoolie Lane reminds us of the scene before Woolworth's extended their premises in 1982 with an entrance to the shop being created where the two doors on the right are seen. Mounthoolie Lane was until c.1900 known as Albert Lane, the name "Mounthoolie" coming from a property to the right of this picture. This view also gives us an excellent idea of the line of the ancient "Lang Gutter" which stretched from the crest of the rise in Laing Street outside the current Orkney Library.

• c.1970 •

This picture, possibly taken c.1970, shows the old lane known as "The Burn" which denoted the line followed by the Papdale Burn on its way to the Peerie Sea after crossing the main street at the Brig. The section shown was in ancient times called the Hempow. The wall on the left separating the gardens of the Bridge Street houses from the lane has now been removed and along with the gardens area has been made into a car park and the road which exits from it and the pavement alongside the Albert Hotel in the direction of "Matchmakers." The tourist office moved at the beginning of the 1980s to Broad Street.

• Late 1970s •

The Brig, the corner of Bridge Street and Albert Street where the Papdale Burn on its way to the Peerie Sea was crossed by a footbridge until about 1850. W. R. Thomson's shop shown here was formerly the old grocery business of J. Maxwell (est. 1879) and is now The Frozen Food Shop. Elliot Forbes, a dry-cleaner's, was once the photograph/records' shop of the well known photographer J. W. Sinclair and is now Sheila Fleet Jewellery. The ship chandlers' shop was that of Nicol Spence & Son (est. 1862) which is now Eccles Insurance Services while Leonards have moved across the Brig and their premises have become Orkney Opportunities Centre.

• c.1966 •

Bridge Street looking north. On the left at the corner is the old established (1879) firm of George Rendall which occupied 1 Albert Street from about 1920. In the 1980s this became J. & J. Smith and in the late 1990s Leonard's booksellers moved into the premises. The junction box beside the telephone kiosk has been removed as has been the water-pump. A post-box now stands in place of the junction-box. On the left side of the street going north is Robert Garden's electrical shop (now Eric Kemp's Sports Shop) and further north the Co-operative shop which is now Business Equipment Service and next door is Jolly's shipbrokers.

This aerial view of Kirkwall taken in the late 1960s is a superb illustration of the former appearance of the town before some massive changes. The road from the left corner is Burnmouth Road and at the junction on the right with Great Western Road is Scarth car sales, car hire and engineering. Across the road a bus stands outside one of Peace's garages which was formerly W. R. Tullock before it moved to Castle Street. Proceeding towards the meeting point with Junction Road on the left is Reynold Johnstone Tyres and Grant's Furniture, the latter of which has now been removed to provide the new car park for the new residential and office block constructed on the site of the buildings at the Kiln Corner, near which can also be seen the petrol pumps at J. T. Miller, cyclists, now the Wireless Museum. The picture also shows the back of all the Bridge Street properties and lanes before the removal of much of the area for another car park. Just below the aircraft wheels is the Burgh Yard which was cleared to create Burgh Road and the car parks on either side of it. The shoreline at Ayre Road, Shore Street and along Cromwell Road before the land reclamation which led to the Shapinsay ferry terminal, the offices and car park etc on Shore Street and the new road layout to Cromwell Road are also prominent.

• Early 1960s •

This scene of Junction Road shows the new Post Office opened in 1960 and next to it is the Cosmo Ballroom. The Post Office was built on the site of Peace's wood yard. The Cosmo was first the site of The Electric Theatre Cinema (1913-28) and during the war was a drill hall. In October 1947 it opened as the ballroom and in November staged the first inter-county dancing versus Shetland. For the next quarter century the "Coser" was to be the mecca of Orkney dancers on Friday and Saturday nights. It then became the Casablanca nightclub and is now Peace's car showroom. The nearest building was demolished to provide the entrance to the Junction Road/Castle Street car park. The walls nearest the camera are now the site of the petrol pumps at W. R. Tullock's garage.

Kirkwall Gas Works. The only reminder of the works which were cleared in April 1980 is the former office seen here. It too was demolished and the area is now the site of the Castleyards housing scheme. The scheme was begun in March 1980 and completed in February 1982.

The Kirkwall Gasworks Company was established in 1838 and was taken over by the Town Council in 1923. Originally the gas provided the public lighting, but from 1923 it was geared to commercial and household use.

• 1980 •

Kirkwall Gas Works. Another angle on the demolition. Beyond the site can be seen Kirkwall Auction Mart which had been there since 1901 though enlarged and changed over the 20th century. Until 1953 it was owned privately but then was purchased by the local farmers. In 1996 it moved to its present complex at Hatston Industrial Estate.

• c.1960 •

Albert Street. In the foreground is the family butcher of James Leith established in 1877 and which had been on this site since 1886. In 1962 the firm moved to occupy the former Bank of Scotland building at the corner of Laing Street, and Horne's butchers, now under J. Miller, took over Leith's premises. The shop is now Donaldson's family butcher. The frontage has been modernised. The shop next (south) is Hourston's Jewellers (c.1866) while next along was D. S. Foubister(1899) whose initials can still be seen on the decorative entrance floor tiles of the premises now occupied by Little Island.

• 1982 •

Retiral of Teddy Tinch. Teddy Tinch worked for James Flett & Sons for well over 60 years, and although he had semi-retired some years previously he still continued to work half-days each day before finally 'hanging up his boots' at the age of 86 in 1982. He is seen here receiving a retirement gift from Arthur Flett on 8th June. The firm itself had traded since 1871, having been founded by James Flett on his return from Canada. The firm occupied 6-12 Bridge Street and sold bread (baked by themselves), confectionery, groceries, ironmongery,

seed, etc. The ironmongers shop which is the furthest door north (left) was a classic with an upstairs gallery running around the four walls. Above the firm name are the windows of part of the shop known as "the ballroom" which is where staff functions were once held. This portion was built over the entrance to the old close called Anchor Close, hence the name Anchor Buildings given to the block. Currently the premises are occupied by a variety of businesses and occupations.

• 1970s •

St Magnus Cathedral Choir. In the late 1960s the choir expanded its activities under its organist Norman Mitchell (front, centre) and also acquired red gowns. In the decades which followed the choir was to produce records and go on tour abroad. Seen here are: Ladies — Alison Munro, Lorna McConnachie, Grace Donaldson, Violet Grieve, Millie Shearer, Rosemary Drever, Molly Hadden, Meg Groat, Tina Leslie, Jessie Sinclair, Christine Stephen, Mimie Firth, Madge Bertram, Thelma Leslie. Men: Dennis Eunson, George Donaldson, George Eunson, David Oddie, Arnold Rendall, Charlie Millar, Jack Donaldson, Alex Stephen, Jimmie Cooper.

• 1987 •

Evie Congregational Board. In March 1987 the Evie Kirk celebrated its centenary over a five-day period including Communion and Thanksgiving services on the Sunday. The church had been opened as a Free Church congregation in 1887 by the Free Kirk minister from South Ronaldsay, thus the Communion and Thanksgiving Services followed the Free Kirk pattern, though the church today is a Church of Scotland Congregation. Evie, which is a linked charged with Rendall and Firth had just welcomed Rev Trevor Hunt to the charge in 1986. Pictured outside the kirk are: Ian Heddle, Billy Wood, Jimmy Work, Edith Sinclair, Davie Miller, David Wood, Rev Trevor Hunt, John Cursiter (Treasurer), Mansie Flaws, Marion Spence, Ronnie Cursiter, George Spence, Alistair Marwick (Clerk), George Stevenson and Jack Stevenson.

• 1982 •

Agricultural Society's County Harvest Home. Agriculture has always been the mainstay of Orkney's economy, and at one time the islands were one of Scotland's crofting counties. Since 1945 many farms have been enlarged through mergers etc. and Orkney is no longer "Crofting." Each year in the autumn following the August "shows" and the crop cutting, harvest homes are held where the trophies won are presented. The county harvest home is one of the biggest events on the social calendar. Pictured here with their trophies are:

back row, George Eunson, Jim Stevenson, Sandy Scarth, Davie Kirkpatrick, Billy Flett, Liam Muir, Jim Baillie, Fred Brown, David Eunson, Charlie Bruce; middle row, Ronald Sinclair, Victor Slater, Jim Anderson, Tommy Flett, Linda Bennett, John Scott, Kenny Eunson, Charlie Merriman, Stewart Wood, John Ravenshear; front row, Craig Spence, Rev. Harald Mooney, Agnes Baillie, Ronnie Baillie, Gladys Leslie, Irene Rendall, Day Wishart, Mary Flett.

Finstown. The delightful village of Finstown, midway between Kirkwall and Stromness, nestles between the Hill of Heddle to the rear and the Rendall Hills at the top of the picture. The village takes its name from an Irish soldier, Phin, who had fought in the Battle of Waterloo, and who settled in Orkney for a time. He built his cottage and opened an inn where the Pomona Inn now stands. The village spread from there to the shore.
On the right can be seen the Oyster Pier used in the early part of the last century when oysters were grown and harvested in the Bay of Firth. In the field behind the church there was a military camp in World War II and some foundations can still be seen. The Grimond housing scheme, built in 1971 and named after the MP 1950-83 who lived in the parish, is now in the fields immediately behind the village. Houses have been built along the Rendall Road. A large part of the sea opposite the cemetery has also been reclaimed.

• 1976 •

Finstown. The advent of an oil terminal at Flotta led to substantial house building on Orkney's main island. Quite a number of Flotta's staff chose to live in Finstown and this picture shows houses being constructed for them off the Heddle Road. Across the bay the white building is the Firth School built in 1937 on the boys' playground of the old school which dated back to 1875. A new Primary School is currently being built on a neighbouring site to the west. It is scheduled to open at the end of 2001.

• 1974 •

Kirking of Kirkwall Town Council. In the days of the town having a council it was a long-established tradition that, following council elections, the new council should be "Kirked" i.e. attend St Magnus Cathedral on the Sunday in May after the election. Reform of local government with emphasis on regionalisation did away with many town councils. This picture shows the last occasion on which the final Kirkwall council was "kirked." Featured are from the left: Tom Sclater (Halberdier); Cllrs Margaret Eunson, Alistair Scholes, James Scott, Clive Thomson (Hon Treasurer), Andrew Wylie (Senior Bailie), Georgina Leitch (Provost), Mr Ronald Robertson (Town Clerk & Burgh Treasurer), Cllrs Robert Munro (Junior Bailie), James Macrae (Dean of Guild), Ernest Donaldson, Robert Leslie, Sybil Roebuck; and Charles Millar (Halberdier).

• Mid-1970s •

The Strynd Houses. The Strynd, known as the King's passage in the days of the Castle, possibly gets its name from the same source as the Strand in London. The houses date from c.1400 but were renovated in 1703. The main house, at the extreme right, was for the Cathedral minister while the next house was the manse of Rev Wm Proudfoot, first minister of the Secession Church (1800). In 1785 Capt John Traill entertained Prince William, Duke of Clarence, the future William IV, in his house in the Strynd. Capt Traill and the Prince were old shipmates. The houses are on the site of the hall of the old Norse earls. In 1978 the houses were again completely renovated and one of the first tenants was Jim Harrison, shoemaker, a stalwart Uppie Ba' player and winner, and maker of the ba's, whose shop had previously been located here.

• Late 1950s •

Broad Street, late 1950s — The buildings seen here are, from the left, the shop of J. & W. Tait (1870), grocer, ironmonger, seed merchant and car sales. With property on Junction Road, one of Orkney's largest firms which has now moved to Hatston The shop is now occupied by Judith Glue Knitwear.

The Town Hall (1884) with offices — Town Clerk etc — on the ground floor, council chamber and main hall on second floor and caretakers flat on the third floor; (after 1975 the Town Hall was totally refurbished and the ground floor offices became the present entrance foyer. The Post Office, on the corner, which had occupied this position since about 1900: (after it moved in 1960 to its current premises, the old office became the Community Centre). J. Tait & Sons, cabinetmakers (1896) which became J. & M. McEwan and then Orkney Television Enterprise.

Kirkness & Gorie dating from at least 1866 when it was just Kirkness. After the firm closed in the early 1980s it had a succession of owners until its present occupiers.

• Late 1960s •

BEA moved to this office in Albert Street in 1956 from 7 Broad Street. This new office had been a chemist shop since 1884 and called Stewart & Heddle from 1903. Boots the Chemists had taken this over in the 1940s. The office is now Ridgway Travel. The British Linen Bank next door opened there for business c.1960. After its merger with the Bank of Scotland in 1971 it had a variety of occupiers before becoming part of D. H. Gorn, drapers, whose main shop was across the street. It is now occupied by Klaize. Note too the "Big Tree" with its railings.

● Late 1960s ●

This view of Kirkwall looking north-east was taken from the roof of the Phoenix Cinema. In the foreground on Junction Road we have two gardens, one with a garage, which were subsequently made into a municipal car park. The garage, walls and structures going left were demolished for the entrance to the car park. The new Salvation Army Hall which opened in the early 1960s is also prominent, but dominating the background landscape is St Magnus Cathedral.

• 1980 •

Retiral of Jackie Bain. After 45 years at sea Jackie Bain, a native of Westray, retired in April. He had joined the Northern Lighthouse Ship *May* in 1938 and in 1946 had joined Orkney Steam on the *Earl Thorfinn* and was steward during its epic voyage in the Hurricane of 1953. He became chief steward on the new *Orcadia* in 1962. He is seen here with his wife Issa at his presentation from his colleagues of what had become Orkney Islands Shipping Company.

Back row, Alistair Learmonth, Albert Towrie, Gary Swanney, Willie Yorston, Tom Drever, John Twatt, Eddie Smith; row two, Robbie Irvine, Douglas Robertson, Benny Norquoy, Tom Towers, Hunter Jamieson, Kenny Bruce, Jimmy King, Ian Learmonth, Bruce Johnston, John Harcus. Row three, Stanley Burgher, John Mears, Rodney Tulloch, Michael Sinclair, Kenny Mackay, Angus Thomson, Kenny Nicholson, Davie Drever.
Front row, Allan Bullen, Jack Scott, Mrs Nan Scott, Capt John Burgher, Mrs Bain, Jackie Bain.

• 1966 •

Kirkwall Harbour. This inner harbour has always been a haven for fishing boats to shelter in when storms blow up and this picture shows a crowded "Basin." The boats here are Danish fishing vessels, and possibly "E" indicates Esjberg. In the background are vessels of the North of Scotland and the Orkney Steam Companies — the *St Magnus* (formerly the *St Clair*, launched in 1936 for the Aberdeen-Lerwick route and then used to replace old *Magnus* in 1960), on the right, and possibly the *St Clement* to the left.

• c.1962 •

The *Orcadia* — this shows the vessel arriving at Kirkwall pier. Diesel-powered she replaced the old steamship *Earl Thorfinn* which had served Orkney's North Isles for the Orkney Steam Navigation Company since 1928. In 1961 the company became the Orkney Islands Shipping Company and is now Orkney Ferries. The *Orcadia* was to serve the isles until her final run on 24th August 1990 when she and the *Islander* were replaced by the new ro-ro vessels *Earl Thorfinn* and *Earl Sigurd*. In the background can be seen the Hatston housing scheme — the former RNAS wartime living quarters which the Town Council acquired in 1952 to provide temporary accommodation for families waiting to move into new council houses. These "huts" were used in this way until 1977.

• c.1960 •

Kirkwall Pier. This view shows the pier on a busy day. Lying off is the *Klydon* owned by Dennison's which operated the Shapinsay-Kirkwall route from 1893 until 1968. In 1969 she sank off Argyll. The *Klydon* succeeded the *Iona* which operated 1893 to 1953. At the right is the *Earl Sigurd* (Orkney Steam). Behind her is the *St Clement* (II), The *Clement* operated Leith-Aberdeen-Orkney. On the east side can be seen the masts of the St Rognvald (III) (North of Scotland Orkney and Shetland Shipping Company) a cargo vessel launched in 1954, the largest ship built by Alexander Hall of Aberdeen. She could carry 280 cattle and 220 sheep. The first *St Rognvald* built in 1883 was wrecked on Burgh Head, Stronsay in 1900. The *St Rognvald* (II) launched in 1901 served Leith-Aberdeen-Orkney-Shetland until 1950 when she was replaced by the *St Ninian*. Both earlier *Rognvalds* were passenger vessels.

• 1973 •

St Rognvald on Thieves Holm. In May 1973 the cargo vessel *St Rognvald* set sail for Aberdeen with five passengers (she could carry just twelve) a consignment of Orkney whisky, 204 cattle and 80 sheep. Bad weather forced her to return to Kirkwall and en route she ran aground on Thieves Holm at the entrance to Kirkwall Bay. The Kirkwall lifeboat *Grace Paterson Ritchie* rescued the passengers but the captain and crew of 14 remained on board to help transfer the livestock via a landing barge to the North Isles ferry, *Islander.* Two weeks later the vessel was refloated by a Dutch salvage vessel, and was eventually able to continue in service.

• 1969 •

• 1969 •

The *Irene*. This ship, registered in Liberia, and with a crew from Greece, wrecked on the shore at Grimness, South Ronaldsay, will be forever associated with the saddest post-war tragedy to hit Orkney — the loss of the Longhope Lifeboat, TGB, on 17th March 1969. The ship left Granton Harbour (near Edinburgh) on Sunday night, 16th, bound for Norway without a cargo. The weather forecast was not favourable, and in Orkney gale force winds lashed the shores for days, whipping the seas into raging huge waves. Finding herself in difficulties on Monday evening the *Irene* fired off red flares which were sighted in South Ronaldsay.

Orkney's lifeboats were alerted and just before 8pm the TGB was launched and headed for the vessel. The TGB was seen by the keepers on the Pentland Skerries at 9.30pm. Then silence. The lifeboat was not seen again until 1.15pm on Tuesday 18th March, upside down. Some time during the night the TGB had capsized and her crew had drowned. Her Coxswain Dan Kirkpatrick and his crew's exploits in saving lives had been

chronicled round the world. Dan had thrice been awarded the Lifeboat Institution's Silver Medal — rescuing the crews of the Aberdeen trawler *Strathcoe* in 1959, the trawler *Ben Barvas* in 1964, the *Ross Puma* in 1968 — the only man alive to hold three silvers. In 1956 he'd been awarded a silver medal from the King of Norway for the part in rescuing 41 crew from the *Dovrefjell*.

The loss of the TGB was a family tragedy. Lost with Dan were his sons Ray and Jack. There was also engineer Robert Johnston and his sons James and Robbie. The others were mechanic Jim Swanson and also Eric McFadyen, who had volunteered at the last minute to make up the crew of eight.

Ironically none of the lifeboats needed to have been launched that night. The *Irene*'s crew were rescued on the shore by the Broughness and Deerness life-saving companies, who fired a rocket line on to the ship and brought the crew to safety.

• 1986 •

Lodge Kirkwall Kilwinning[38] office-bearers. This picture was taken in the lodge-room to celebrate the 250th anniversary of the local masonic lodge, one of the oldest in Scotland. Freemasonry has a long history and modern Freemasonry arose out of the interest in the philosophies of the 17th century linked with the old practical or operative craft of stonemasons, who built the great edifices of medieval times. In their localities Freemasons have been responsible for many acts of charity and beneficence, albeit always done quietly without fuss or publicity, and at one time used to carry out a ceremonial laying of foundation stones of important buildings e.g. the Town Hall and their own hall in Kirkwall in 1884. Back row, Clifford Stephen, John Robertson, Freddie Rorie, Alistair Kelday, Raymond Stanger, Raymond Rendall, Balfour Wylie, Sammy Gorn; row two, David Partner, Colin Corse, George Harcus, Jack Kelday, George Moncrieff, Tom Budge, Tom Tullock, Charles Millar, John Corse; seated, Jack Donaldson, George Miller, Norn Donaldson, Archie Firth, David Bain (Master), Arnold Rendall, Donald Ritchie, George Blance.

• 1986 •

The Eastern Star was founded in America in 1850 for the female relations of Master Masons in Freemasonry by Dr Robert Morris. Despite this connection it is not a masonic or quasi-masonic institution, though men masons can join. Kirkwall's Chapter was founded in April 1954. This picture was taken on the second occasion that Mrs Nan Macrae became chairperson. Pictured are; front row, Bella Spence, Edith Laird, Violet Louttit, Nan Macrae, Helen Muir, Maureen Dennison, Jean Skinner, Rena Kelday; row two, Mary Robinson, Edna Stephen, Mildred Bradshaw, Dorothy Little, Gwen Sinclair, Margaret Brennan, Ida Wylie, Betty Stewart, Zan Drever, Edith Pirie, Helen Manson, Mabel Mackintosh; back rows, Mimie Sclater, Annie Sinclair, Kathleen Daniels, Ivy Harcus, Lawrence Daniels, Mabel Kemp, Isobel Ryrie, Iris MacBeath, Ann Linklater, Kathleen Murray, Mary Flett, George Harcus, Stephen Manson Jim Macrae, Bella Findlay, Elizabeth Findlay, Clara Kirkpatrick, Lilian Stephen, Muriel Groat, Ian Sinclair, Irene Campbell, Glenda Solloway, Lily Findlay, Marion Down.

• 1960s •

Clay Loan. This picture from c.1964 shows the bottom of Clay Loan and its junctions with Laverock Road and Main Street on the left, Victoria Street on the right, its extension of Union Street and in the distance Junction Road, known to all locals as the "Back Road." Note the milk-vending machine on the left and the wall round the electricity sub-station. There is a fine view of Tom Brass' shop in the gable facing up Clay Loan. Quite a number of changes have occurred here. The milk-machine has gone, as Brass' shop to widen Union Street, and flats have been created with the gable next to Brass' shop.

The Clay Loan was anciently the "south loan" or "common loan" and its modern name arises from the fact that the old houses were built of clay. At the head of the loan stood Kirkwall's gallows. Laverock Road came into existence with the first post-1945 houses and commemorates the "Laverock," the area of the town which was the domain of the bishop from the palace southwards. Another street parallel to Laverock Road, called Broadsands, refers to that particular stretch of the sands of Kirkwall shore running from 79 Victoria Street to the Clay Loan.

• 1964 •

Tom Brass' shop interior. This shop was established in 1895 and served generations of Kirkwallians, especially those living at the south end of Victoria Street, Main Street, Clay Loan etc but also many others, who made a point of heading for the shop. For schoolboys from the south end of the town, from High Street etc, it was a port of call going to and from school. Here we see Mrs Brass and her son Magnus (grandson of Tom) in the shop. Notice the produce on the shelves and the large sweet-jars on the counter, the latter a common feature in all the old grocer shops. This shop was demolished and the west part renovated into the flats currently on the site.

Acknowledgements

Dougie Shearer has been a 'weel-kent' figure in Kirkwall, in fact in Orkney, most of his life through the wide sphere of interests in which he has been involved – cinema, dance-bands, photography, to name but a few. His family before him had a long association with public events and productions. When James Miller, managing editor/director of *The Orcadian* asked me to write the captions for "a book of Dougie's photos we're publishing" it did not take too long consideration to say "yes." I had known of, and been acquainted with, Dougie all my life, especially through a life-long friendship with one of his nephews, and through going to the *Phoenix* and the *Cosmo* in my youth.

I have had a great deal of pleasure in researching material for the captions and have learned further information to add to my store of knowledge about Kirkwall in particular and Orkney in general. Even on the few better days of summer we had, I still enjoyed being inside following up more clues and leads for the captions which I hope will prove interesting to the readers of this book.

I am deeply indebted to a variety of sources and a large number of people for the information in the captions. *Peace's Almanac*, articles from *The Orkney View*, Roddy Hibbert's material in the museum, and in particular Hossack's *Kirkwall in the Orkneys* and Howard Hazell's *The Orcadian Book of the 20th Century* all provided leads and sometimes full information to assist me. The archive staff in the County Library are also due thanks for all their assistance. There are over fifty members of the public who assisted – especially in identifying people in the photographs – too many to name individually. But while all of them made me most welcome – and I did appreciate the time they spent, no matter how minimal – some are perhaps due a special thanks: Sandy Firth for identifying even the smallest boats in the Basin and some aspects of KGS (not forgetting Alistair Cormack and Jimmie Dewar in those items too); Jack Muir for the Stromness aspects; my former colleague Jocky Wood for Finstown; Rev Trevor Hunt for Evie Kirk; Leslie and Grace Tait, various members of the TA, Fred Croy for the Flying Club, Ken Ross, Brian Kemp, Lydia Campbell, Margaret and Arthur Flett, Alan Clouston and the several members of the Eastern Star. And of course James Miller whose editorial and publishing expertise kept me right on what would be interesting reading for the public.

Every attempt has been made to be accurate with names and dates. Dougie did not record dates of shots. A process of deduction and logic using clues from the photos and use of memory, as well as news items in the Press have, I hope, given accurate approximations for the photos where no specific date could be obtained. Any mistakes in dates or names are my fault.

This is however Dougie Shearer's book. His photographs are the all-important item. They represent Dougie's wide interests. They reflect the changing scenes his camera has recorded. They are a lifetime's work. My contribution is a mere three months work, a drop in the ocean of time Dougie has spent recording events and people through the eye of a camera. I hope the book will prove an enjoyable addition to the library of Orkney books now available.

David Partner